Songs from the Territories

Songs from the Territories

and other works of photography, poetry, narrative

Chaim Bezalel

DEKEL
PRESS

This edition was produced for on-demand distribution by iUniverse.com, Inc.
for Dekel Press.
iUniverse.com, Inc.
620 North 48th St., Suite 201
Lincloln, NE 68504
www.iUniverse.com

For information address:
Dekel Press
1754 Pacific Drive
Camano Island, WA 98282
(800) 898-4998
www.bezalel-levy.com

ISBN: 0-595-13694-X

Printed in the United States of America

to my sons— Ezra, George, and Sam

Contents

Introduction	9
Songs from the Territories	13-23
Architectural Elements	25-39
Hamsin (East Wind)	41-55
On the Pursuit of Happiness	57-58
Songs of Exile	59-75
Observations on the Border	77-103
In the Public Domain	105-111
Workaday Verse	113-119

Introduction

What is it that gives birth to a nation? Is it as simple as Theodore Hertzl put it? "If you will it, it is not a dream." Is it indeed simple to mobilize the will of a people? Is nationalism an outmoded, 19th century Romantic concept, a dangerously potent mixture of "blood and earth?" Must a nation be birthed in blood? Are the nations which were chartered in the early 20th century by a group of old men at a conference table at Versailles really nations, or are the tribal factions that are tearing these nations apart the true nations?

In the past, sovereign rights were adduced by Divine Right or Manifest Destiny. Territory has usually been the spoil of war. Federal republics, whether dictatorial or democratic, have arisen, imposing the dominant ethnic and ideological priorities on their amalgamated, sometimes conquered populations.

Israel, in defining itself in its Declaration of Independence as a Jewish State, must be ready to deal with the ramifications of this definition. The world is converting to a new paradigm, a new catholicity, a secular one, in which the media is father confessor, sometimes inquisitor. This pax romanus is set against notions of tribal exclusivity, mission, and choseness, which have always been both a blessing and a curse, particularly for the Jewish State, whether that state has been physical, mystical, or psychological.

These poems and essays were written primarily over a five year period, from 1991 through 1995, beginning during the Gulf War when, as a recent citizen of Israel, I was inducted into the army reserves for basic training. I am not sure whether my conclusions have changed during this time or if my thoughts have become more inconclusive. As the poet and playwright Heinrik Ibsen wrote in a letter: "The task of the poet is to make clear to himself, and thereby to others, the temporal and eternal questions."

Songs from the Territories

I
Prologue

Which part of wisdom is prophecy
and which the implementation?
Joseph in prison, to Pharaoh's cupbearer said:
"It is God given, the dream's interpretation.
In three days you shall be free,
but the baker shall be dead."
And so it came to pass exactly as interpreted,
that the baker was hanged, and the butler set free;
and Joseph cried after him, "Remember me!"

- Winter 1971, Catskill, New York

II

Redemption happens slowly.
Four hundred years till Joseph's bones
are brought up to Shechem, a holy site to the Jews.
Shrewd as he was, enslaving all Egypt
for their own grain, he knew
the ground around his remains
was bound to appreciate.
Location is the vocation;
occupation the occupation.

- Winter 1991, Ba'ad Arba (closed in 1995)
Basic Training Camp adjoining Beit El settlement

III

I am writing this on a rifle butt,
where Jacob dreamed of angel's visitations -
a ladder ascends into the bunker hut.
"This is the house of God, and I knew it not,"
they read at the initiation, and handed me a gun.
Is this the implementation?
Is this the iron rod,
which even the prince of peace must wield
upon this planet?

- Ba'ad Arba

IV

From here we face west toward Jerusalem.
From this crest above jewel encrusted hills,
it seems vast, the land possessed
with the hyperbole of the East.
As I passed the little shul, a gun slung on my breast,
the Sabbath had begun, the day of rest,
and I noticed, pressed against the western wall
toward the setting sun, stood the Holy Ark,
which caught my interest
because, child of the West, it seemed to me reversed.
This is the other facet, like the dark side of the moon
or a diamond compressed by untold heat
and time, and by earth impressed.
This stone will not be cut
In Antwerp or Amsterdam, New York or Tel Aviv;
nor can the hand of any man stand the test.

- February 1992, Ba'al Hazor
   (highest point in Judean mountains)

V

fog in the darkness
sky meets mountains
borders ill defined
and I am a twig
fallen in the stream
past stone walls and terraced hills
a stream like other streams
a twig like other twigs
the lights on the horizon
could be any ghost city of the night
another night another month
in the territories
in the watchtower
the wind whistles repetitiously
like a flute in the casbah
nothing is happening here
that meets the naked eye
in the telescope
barbed wire squiggles on the fence
like arabic script
celestial forces at large
struggle surreptitiously
beyond the searchlights penetration
for destinies of nations
the skies are charged tonight
lighting instead of missiles

- Ba'al Hazor

VI

Swirling snowflakes stream into the vortex,
caught in the searchlight, streaking
like a time exposure of a starry sky -
but it is we who are suspended.
The watchtower becomes a rocket-ship
as time slows...stops....changes direction.
Staring out the window of a subway train
at the windows of another train passing
in the opposite direction,
I would let mind loose for a moment,
forget my destination, and abandon myself
to the sensation, brought on by motion's
relativity that it was we who were traveling
in the opposite direction.
I feel myself atomizing until I
am not really I, but anonymous,
the eye of the storm.
We are snowbound, curfewed,
marooned on this mountain -
no one arrives no one leaves the base.
We are impregnable as the Russian winter
against Napoleon or worse.
Yet, last week as I wrote a verse
on Sabbath rest, soldiers on another base
were hacked to death in the sleeping bags.
And when I thought only lightning was hurled,
a missile fell on a little girl;
and the wind which whistled like a flute
now howls like a thousand screaming mullahs.

- *Ba'al Hazor*

This is the house of God, and I knew it not

the land possessed with the hyperbole of the East

sky meets mountains

the lights on the horizon could be any ghost city of the night barbed wire squiggles on the fence like Arabic script

We are snowbound

We are impregnable as the Russian winter

Architectural Elements

I

Is it certainty that breeds elegance?
That the world is ordered?
That this order is manifest?
Symmetry of purpose and execution.
Beware, beauty is its own reward,
unencumbered by truth.
But what is truth without conviction,
or conviction without truth?
The former, inconsequent,
the latter, destruction.
We see the husks
scattered through the countryside,
decomposing on the ground
like fruit past season,
ideas whose time has come and gone,
whose seeds do sometime spring again.

II

Elements of Arabic architecture,
each altogether suggestive
of some hidden pleasure:
the Dome of the Breast;
the Arch of the Torso;
the minaret's preeminence;
the interplay of prurience and prudery,
revelation and concealment,
a dance of seven veils or Sheharazade's
tales within tales.
As she herself regales
quoting another source,
both more ancient and anonymous:

"Guard thy secret from another, intrust in not;
for he who intrusteth a secret has lost it."
This from *The Ladies of Baghdad*.
To which the facile tongued porter
meets aphorism with metaphor:
"A secret is with me is as a house with a lock,
whose key is lost and whose door is sealed."
Thus gaining entrance to the harem,
he seduces them with song and wine
to the end - well ...
one must enter into the nautilus shell.

III

My lover dreams of houses,
and dreams they are images of herself,
a mutable interior, a stage set, struck
and then rearranged in endless variations
both familiar and strange:
First House of Matrimony;
Abode of Adolescence;
The Summer Cabin.
For her, structure was everything.
Gutted, ripped from the foundation,
she was, however, able to retain
some of the furniture,
passed down for generations.
Whereas I salvaged nothing but experience,
and so I dream of conversations, confrontations, visitations
and restorations.
We all have our dark side,
though some seek out the familiar
and others the strange.
Does not beauty contain a touch of ugliness
to keep it from the mundane?

a mutable interior
Safed

Elements of Arabic architecture
Fountain, Jerusalem

Symmetry of purpose and execution
Turkish Bath, Acco

We see the husks
Abandoned Structure, Ashkelon

scattered through the countryside
Demolished Structure, Tel Aviv

the Dome of the Breast
Sheik's Tomb, Kochav Yair

the Arch of the Torso
Abandoned Structure, Ashkelon

the mineret's preeminence
Jaffa

A secret with me is as a door with a lock
Jaffa

One must enter
Interior of Mineret, Ashkelon

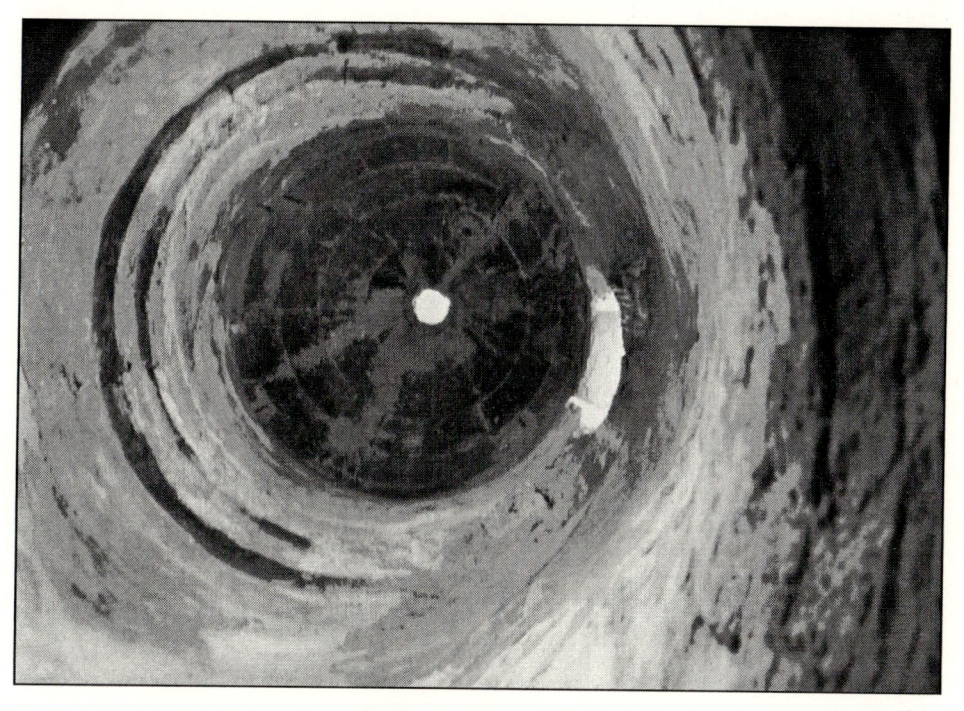

into the nautilus shell
Interior of Mineret, Ashkelon

Hamsin (East Wind)

I

The east wind brings ill tidings
called hamsin, sharaav, sirocco,
a desert wind, a gritty wind
penetrating the nostrils,
filling the mouth to the back teeth.
It is better not to speak.
The mind reels, inflamed,
caught under a magnifying glass.
An east wind parted the Red Sea,
"the wind of judgment,"
a commentator called it.

A shift in atmosphere is detected
as the weather forecast fades
into a sandstorm of white noise.
The weatherman's voice remains calm
even as it is overcome
by the words of the Prophet.
A change in temperature,
if not government,
is in the offing.
Out of Egypt the reception comes
clear as a bell.
Switch to drama of mustachioed physiognomy
caught in outcry of outraged honor-
Cut to woman peering through the curtain,
mascara applied to hieroglyphic eyes.
Ashkelon tributary once more,
outmost outpost of Asia,
the incontinent continent
that perfected both pleasure and torture,
twin pursuits of the true sensualist.
It is an east wind that shrivels the will
and subjugates it to the god of forces,
the Prince of Persia, who restrained

even the Archangel for a time,
or times, or half a time.
Then it lifts, followed by a west wind,
a sea wind, a freshening wind,
a soothing upon the land.

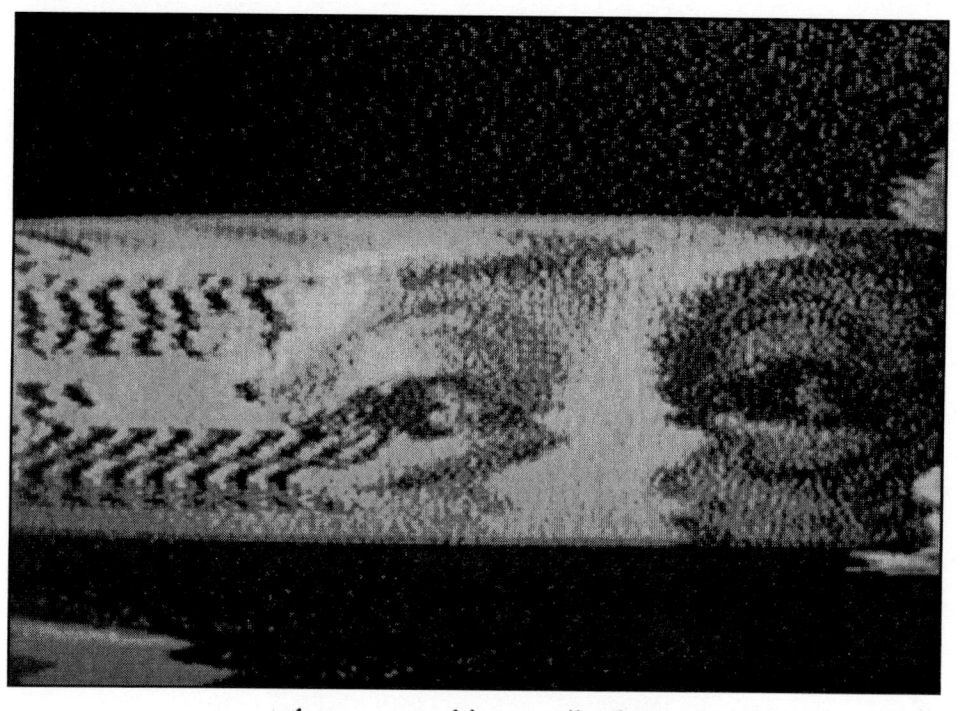

The east wind brings ill tidings

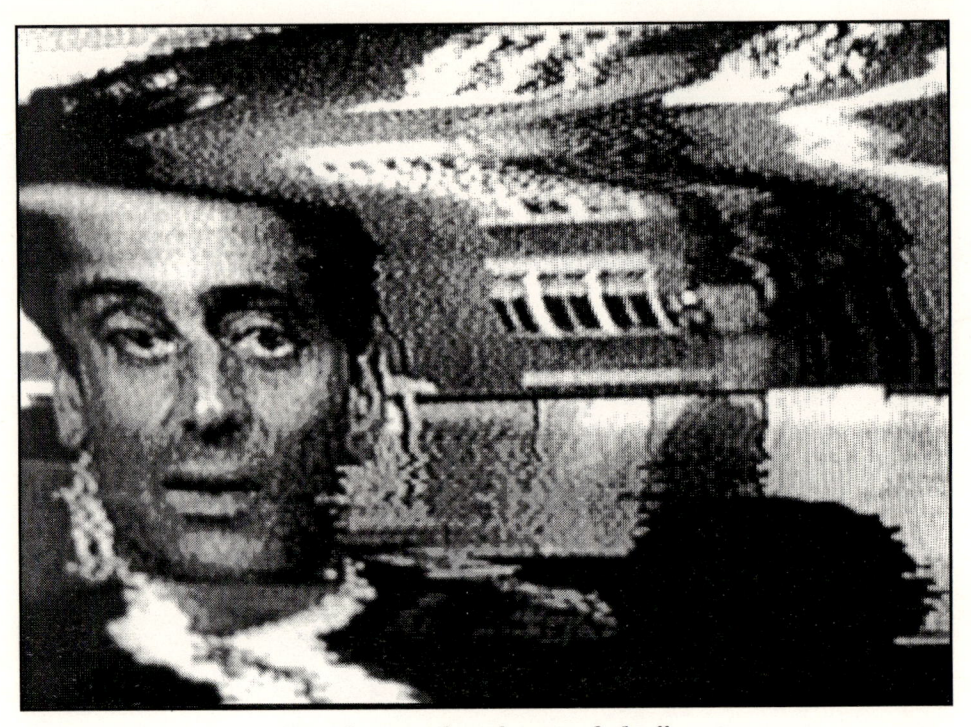

"as the weather forcast fades"

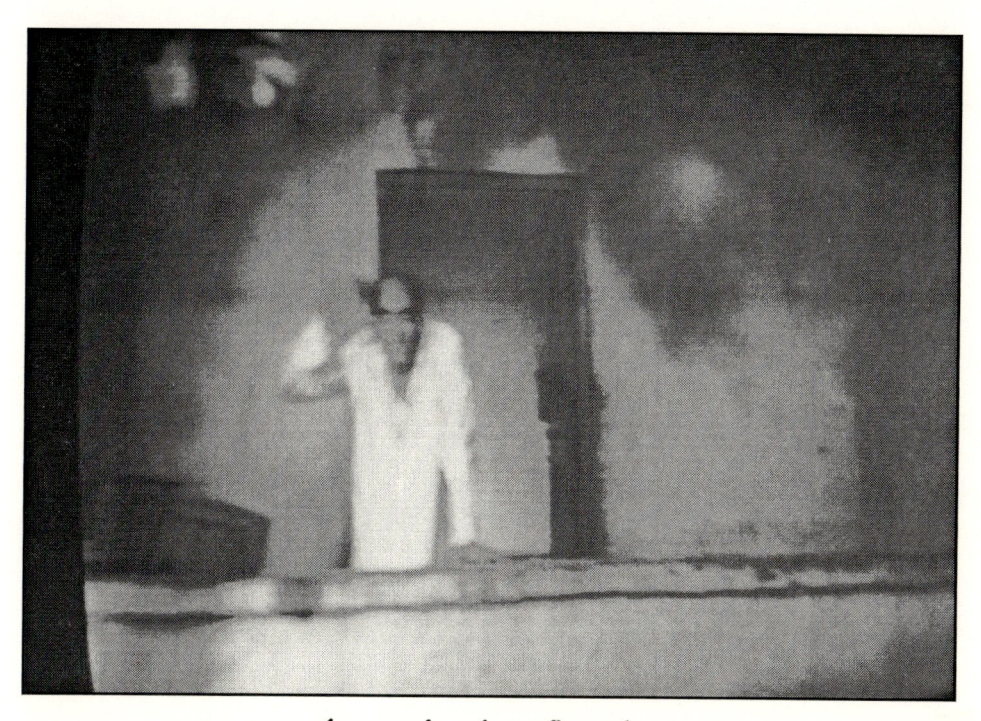

the mind reels, inflamed

Out of Egypt the reception comes clear as a bell.

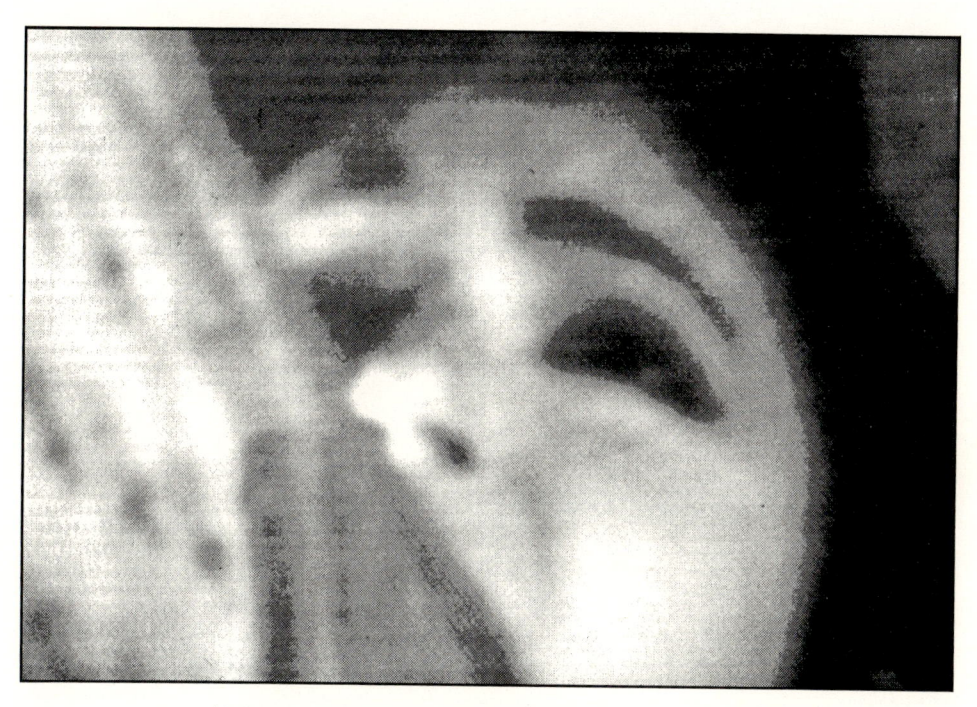

"Cut to woman peering through the curtain"

twin pursuits of the true sensualist

Ashkelon tributary once more

It is an east wind that shrivels the will

II

I dreamed I was walking to Germany,
back to autumn's quiet harmony.
It was 1938, before it was too late,
before I was even born.
This October is an incinerator,
like the depths of Levantine summer.
But I turned back to my parched land,
brown, awaiting first rain like kisses
after a lover's long absence;
and I knew the word *repentance*
means abandonment to the deepest truth
which, though sensed,
shows only its back as it passes
like a dream.

- October 1993, after returning to Israel from Germany

I dreamed I was walking to Germany

back to autumn's quiet harmony

On the Pursuit of Happiness

At what point in a culture does the pursuit of happiness become a guiding principle? Somewhere beyond mere survival. The pursuit of happiness is not an indulgence, nor inherently decadent, though it can become so. It is the very essence of liberty. Of course there can be no guarantee that we will achieve happiness, only that we may pursue it. The paradox is that happiness comes only with the submission of oneself to something larger than oneself, but, like love, it cannot be coerced.

Art, for better or worse, has become the preeminent expression of the pursuit of liberty and happiness. Personal creativity is like an eternal spring which cannot be quenched, though that has often been often tried. Even in the concentration camps all of the arts were pursued despite everything. This proves that it is a basic human need, like food and sex, not a mere luxury. It also demonstrates that freedom exists primarily in the mind.

It is no coincidence that the Impressionist movement (which released artists from the tyranny of religion and state in that it was the first non-heroic, that is to say non- propagandistic, movement) emerged amidst the political struggle to establish true democracy in France during the reign of the self-styled emperor, Napoleon III. It is also no surprise that what seems innocuous and pretty to us today, caused riots and charges of immorality when it was first exhibited. It was correctly perceived as a threat to the authoritarian view of the body politic, where even art was under the control of bureaucrats. Today it is generally acknowledged that art or literature in the service of anything other than its own integrity is not art. It may be advertising, or propaganda, or entertainment, or even good design, but it does not deal directly with the essence of liberty which is the individual's right to the pursuit of happiness.

I am jotting down these thoughts while doing reserve duty as a guard in a prison camp for Palestinian prisoners. I, who do not like confinement of any kind, coming from a non-authoritarian culture, having come of age in an antiauthoritarian era, do not find the army, or prison, conducive to my happiness. Yet, at the same time, having come from a country which has never been invaded since 1812 to one which is invaded periodically, acknowledge the need for a standing army. Were it not for the strong civilian element, with the reserves supplying a good deal of the forces, the army could well have become insulated from the public. It could have become the cult it is in many xenophobic dictatorships. On the other hand, an all volunteer army is one of the classic elements of an empire. So, it is with the hope of being phased out, counting the days, with the greatest appreciation of the importance of maintaining and enlarging my right to the pursuit of happiness, that I serve.

– Prison Camp #7, in the Negev Desert - December 1993

Songs of Exile

"Exile is the dream of glorious return."
—Salman Rushdie
from *The Satanic Verses*

Prison Camp #7, Negev Desert

I

Funny that I, who might have found myself
    in jail in another place and time,
Come halfway around the world
    to serve a prison guard -
Certainly a punishment to fit the crime.
They, down in the prison yard,
    pacing like leopards in a cage -
I, a captive audience in the tower,
    observing them hour by hour.
I always suspected that
    the jailer's incarcerated too.
In a broader sense, the question's who
    is in his natural habitat?
And if both of us, then who's the mouse
    and who's the cat?

II

A mouse runs into the prison yard.
It is surrounded.
The circle tightens.
What will they do?
The guards line up to see.
Will they let it go?
Someone squeezes its tail with a squeegee.
Will they keep it for a pet?
Another ties its tail with a strip of rag.
It tugs and tugs.
He picks it up and swings it around.
Will he fling it to freedom?
Someone gets some paper and lights it.
The mouse is dipped into the flame.
Over and over.
It is taken away, still alive.
I stop watching.

III

One might wonder what act
I committed prior to this flight,
not of fancy, but in fact,
what indiscretion or oversight,
and was its collar black or white?
Responding with utmost tact,
I admit that I was lax
and failed to file income tax.
In the end it's a matter of loyalty,
rendering to God and to Caesar their dues
respective of the deity or royalty
by which we are chosen or happen to choose.

IV

A certain man had two sons.
One son he prepared for sacrifice,
And ever since, that son
Has felt himself a victim.
His other son the man cast out
Into the desert
Without sufficient water or provision.
Miraculously, that son, too, survived.
Two sons, both traumatized -
One doesn't want to be a victim anymore.
    The other doesn't want to be an outcast anymore.

V

Sometimes I feel like ontogeny
    recapitulating phylogeny,
Moving backwards through stations
    of my father's immigration,
    but in the opposite direction.
Perhaps my ultimate rejection was
    in embracing all that he transcended;
Or perhaps, in exile my exile is ended,
    and in going I am returning.
The prodigal progeny.

VI

"Are you a new immigrant?" a young
    prisoner asks.
"Not new, but yes."
"Welcome," he bids in the Hebrew tongue.
And I am tempted to guess,
To your land or mine?
Israel or Palestine?

VII
Ethics of the Fathers

Abraham pimped for his wife
to save his own life.
Isaac tried the same
but got caught at the game.
Jacob was a schemer,
Joseph, a dreamer,
so his brothers sold him for a slave.
Moses hid his corpse in a shallow grave
before jumping the border.
David had it done in order
to steal the victim's wife.
Solomon had a thousand in his life,
a harem more magnificent than Suleiman.
And such were our holy men,
not that they weren't,
if sometimes their behavior was a little aberrant.

VIII

In the tent, eight candles are alight -
Chanukah, the Feast of Dedication.
Meanwhile, the very night,
The exiles arrive from Lebanon.
Three busloads, windows painted white,
Leaders of Hamas, their zealous priests.
We line up in tight formation,
Rifles at the ready,
Searchlights streaming, cameras rolling
Like a Hollywood opening night.
Later, it appears on the eight o'clock news
Followed by a piece
on the Temple Mount Faithful,

Neo-Maccabees wanna kindle candles
On the ancient site.
No great miracle happened here tonight.

IX

Romanticism kills.
It is by nature a lost cause,
A longing for what was, or never was,
And cannot be fulfilled.

Unconsummated, it must
Remain, a search for a Grail
Which is bound to fail,
Lest it be revealed just dust.

Stylized with certain conventions:
The quest; the code; the creed;
Saladin or Galahad upon the white steed,
Life imitating art in endless declensions.

How willingly we suspend our disbelief
Like Don Quixote for his blessed whore,
In his eyes virgin evermore.
But every lie must come to grief.

Perhaps I'm wrong, I may be,
And a troubadour from time to time
Reminds us love is not a crime,
Nor a matter of degree.

X

Call me Gershom,
    a stranger in a strange land.
Call me Menassah,
    for I have forgotten my father's house.
Call me Maher-shalal-hash-baz,
    hasten booty hasten spoil.
Call me Mara, the bitter one.
Call me Benoni, son of sorrow and toil.
Call me Cain, behold a man,
    an exile and an exile's son.
And what of the sons whom I begot
    back in Babylon, Egypt, or was it Rome?
Will they forget; I will not.
And one question I ask of God:
Is this the land of honey or the land of Nod?

XI

The radio plays
Silent Night in Arabic -
"All is calm, all is bright"
    by halogen light.
"Dreams are like angels"
    they sing on the air.
Down below, an achromatic trill
    startles me, the call to prayer.
And I think of you sleeping still
    beyond the faint shimmering
lights of Beersheba.
"Morning will come; morning will come"
the radio prophesies in song.
And in that day, a woman
    shall compass about a man.

You painted the picture,
    the tiger resting in the grass
while the tigress stands watch above.
But now I watch till dawn, my love.

XII
Exile of Speech

Let me spill my ink upon the page
    and leave this web of words
        this cold exile of living.
The world is not my cup of tea.
Will you be my mother, lover, sister, nurse?
I will be your father, brother, friend, wise man, little boy.
Now, if we fold the paper
    and let it bleed - tell me
        what do you see?

XIII
Memoirs of the Diaspora

A borrowed view of borrowed trees
    against a borrowed sky.
Memories of childhood.
Torch songs left over from the war
    overheard on the radio.
Somebody else's love story,
    maybe mommy and daddy's.
They gave me a name
borrowed from Celtic lore,
Another from a dead cousin-once-removed,
Who shared it with the emperor
    of the Holy Roman Empire.

This was my identity, notwithstanding
that when attached to the family moniker,
Hastily adopted some years back
    to aid the Czar's conscription,
It became nearly as unpronounceable
    as the tetragrammaton.
Borrowed heirlooms
from earlier immigrations,
Secured for consideration,
    adorned our home.
Retrospectively, taken collectively,
    despite all the activity,
The years of my family's sojourn on that shore
Have not been much more than seventy,
About the span of the Babylonian Captivity.

XIV
Epilogue

I mourn the loss of frontier.
It is what keeps us sane.
Without it, we go out to convert the world
To our collective god or brand name.
Not that everyone should live there,
Just that it exists,
Something as yet unspoiled, bare
Of all but necessity.
I mourn the loss of frontier,
Where the outcast, outlaw, fortune seeker
Can have a clean slate
With inducement to settle and cultivate.

to serve as a prison guard

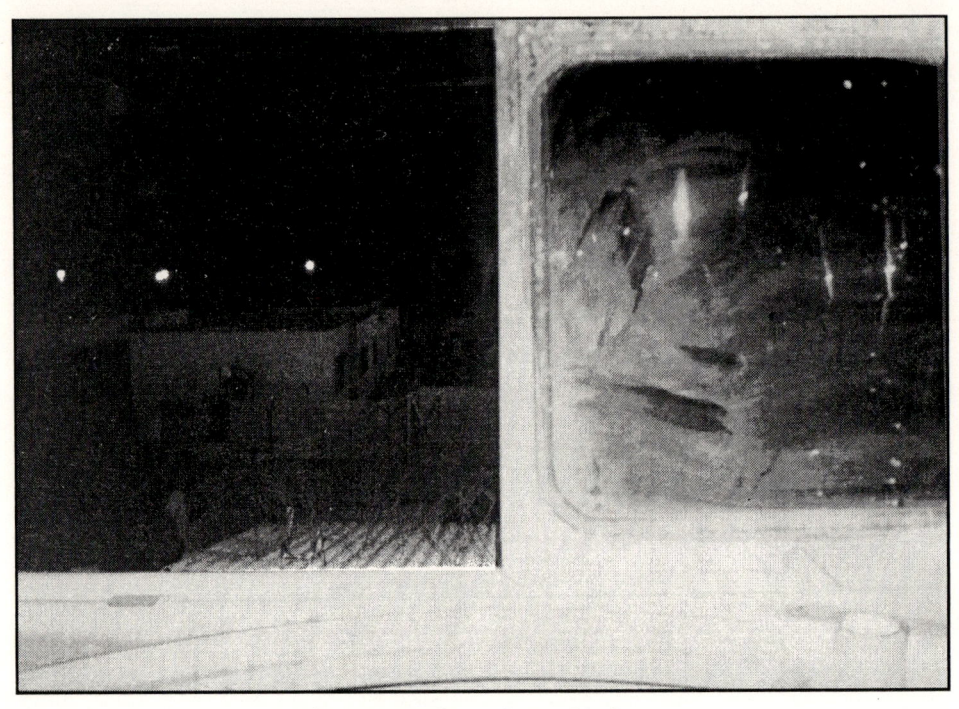

observing them hour by hour

pacing like leopards in a cage

"Dreams are like angels"

they sing on the air

"Morning will come; morning will come."

this cold exile of living

Observations on the Border

*"... in any country anywhere
 whose boundaries and rivers are uncertain"*

–Rainer Maria Rilke
From a Stormy Night VI

This will be my final posting in the reserves. We "old men," 45 and over, are being phased out, put in the "deep freeze," to give a literal translation. But first, my last stand, patrolling a rather isolated and arbitrary line in the sand, which was negotiated in 1909 between the Ottoman Turkish Empire and the British Empire, then protectors of Palestine and Egypt respectively. To the west of this line, the Negev, to the east, the Sinai - extensions of the same desert, but in the middle of July it seems as if each contributes its own sun.

The spiky shrubs look like iron filings arrayed in a magnetic field, but at night, under multitudinous stars and frequent shooting stars, the probing searchlight reveals each shrub transformed from iron gray to lush, succulent green. As we negotiate our open jeep along the stony path, crawling up mountains and down into the valleys, I let my mind drift through the six hour border patrols. There are two others with me in the jeep, a radio man and a Bedouin tracker who recognizes every fresh mark in the sand. The path is raked daily by trucks dragging rolls of barbed wire. The three of us can change a flat in five minutes, a daily occurrence due to the preponderance of barbs which break off from the wire. Sometimes on the mountain top or down in the dunes, we stop and the tracker prepares coffee on an open fire.

I am doing a lot of thinking about borders. The big difference between real and imaginary borders is that real ones need to be acknowledged by one's neighbors and validated by the larger community, whereas imaginary ones need only to be ascertainable to participants and to interested spectators, like boundaries in a sporting event. During the two thousand years of the Diaspora, the Jews existed within the countries of exile in a borderless state, a state within a state, complete with its own body of laws.

The traditional view is that the lack of boundaries was the very thing that kept Judaism alive after the destruction of the Temple and the subsequent dispersion of the Jews. When Yochanon Ben Zaccai was given permission by the Romans to establish a yeshiva at Yavne, he was asked by his disciples, "What do we do now that the Temple is destroyed?" He answered, "We learn about it." In other words, we sublimate; we live vicariously.

Three daily prayer services replaced and adopted the names of the three daily sacrifices. Yet, this provisional condition was never intended to be permanent, and prayers were also recited, such as the one included in the blessing after every meal, for the rebuilding of the Temple in Jerusalem.

The borderless state proved most efficacious as long as the presiding ruler was magnanimous. Often, though, the lack of borders proved threatening to all concerned. In reaction, the Jews constructed an ever more restrictive "hedge around the law," fortifying the interior boundaries, and their Gentile neighbors built more concrete boundaries in the form of ghettos. For better or worse, Jews existed in an imaginary, or canonical kingdom for thousands of years; but that entire way of life has ultimately been discarded by the vast majority, both in Israel and the Diaspora. The question is, what will replace it?

Thankfully, a season of revival always follows the season of dormancy, morbidity, stultification, and chill, as surely as spring follows even the longest winter. Judaism is like a very old tree; it has survived a long time. The reason is that it is organic and flexible, a complex mixture of people, place, and history. Perhaps, it may be defined as the relationship among the people of Israel, the land of Israel, and the God of Israel, or, some might say, the Law of God. It is that potent mixture of blood and earth, which the worst of our enemies, such as the Nazis, have tried to counterfeit in their most mystic rites. This cult of blood and earth, which lies at the foundation of Judaism, is indeed a mystical phenomenon; it cannot be fully explained. However, it must be tempered by the third phenomenon, namely God, or the Law, or even by "ethical culture."

Nevertheless, Judaism divorced from the land of Israel is simply not Judaism. This connection of land and religion may also exist in other national churches such as Greek or Russian Orthodoxy or Anglicanism, wherein the monarch is, at least titularly, "protector of the faith," but in Judaism there is yet a deeper layer, beyond tradition, and that is the Bible itself. The Bible specifies the Land of Israel as inimical to the destiny of the Jews. The religious issue is unavoidable, though highly embarrassing to the modern mind. Yet it is the Bible which underlies the modern mind with its multi-dimensional characterization of individuals, just as it underlies our entire concept of history – and not only for the Jews. The written history and hence the very nationhood and even the language of many countries began with their translation of the Bible. History can be perceived as the story of borders.

A hundred and fifty years ago, when America expanded westward and, to put it mildly, dispossessed the Indians, the doctrine of Manifest Destiny claimed that it was the will of God for the nation to expand and to Christianize the continent. This was the "democratic" version of the doctrine of Divine Right. Today such excuses are no longer credible. Witness how the Serbian doctrine of "ethnic cleansing" was received by the community of nations.

Still, any organism will sooner or later want to probe its boundaries, especially if they have been overly restrictive, though this exploration does not always end with positive results. Some parts fall away, or die, but in the end it militates toward the health of the complete organism. This is exactly what is taking place today as questions are resolved about the existence of Israel and its boundaries, both spiritual and physical.

Zionism, even in its secular form, has been a revivalist movement, basically religious in nature. If this were not the case, then it has already fulfilled its mandate to establish a Jewish state in the land of Israel, along with all of the accouterments of statehood including an indigenous army, language, and culture, all of the functions for which government ministries exist. Therefore, if Zionism is not basically religious in nature, longing for an ultimate transcendent reality, then it has become just another nationalist movement, perhaps chauvinistic, at worst jingoistic. This is the accusation of its enemies and the fear of many disillusioned Zionists, including Israelis. At the Hebrew University in Jerusalem, the chairman of the German studies department is reported to have said: "If we fear right-wing radicalism, the Tenach (Bible) ought to be banned. The linkage of literature with politics is more menacing than *Mein Kampf.*"[1]

The mixture of religion and politics is frightening to modern secularists, regardless of so-called "religious preference." This fear has been more than borne out by the recent assassination of Rabin. Nevertheless, I believe that Zionism is basically a religious movement whose ultimate goal is not only the ingathering of the entire Jewish people, but its transformation as well. Many would argue, "Well, perhaps not the *entire* Jewish people. The Diaspora has an important role to play." The early Zionists, looking back on various persecutions and maybe even sensing the impending Holocaust doubted that the Diaspora would even continue to exist in the long run. But it has continued and prospered and has contributed its own multifarious version, its own vernacular.

In an advertisement in an American Jewish magazine, a singer published some of the lyrics to her song inspired by Psalm 137. The original psalm goes:

"By the rivers of Babylon, there we sat down, yea, we wept, when we remembered Zion.

We hanged our harps upon the willows in the midst thereof. For there they that carried us away captive required of us a song; and they that wasted us required of us mirth, saying, 'Sing us one of the songs of Zion..'

How shall we sing the LORD's song in a strange land?"

The revisionist version begins: "By the waters of the *Hudson*, we *picked up* our harps." Of course this is an extreme example of cosmopolitanism as compared to the particularism of a small religion operating in a small country. In the extreme, particularism becomes a cult while cosmopolitanism becomes a social club.

One of my fellow reservists asked me, "What do we (Israelis) do better than anybody else?" He was expecting me to answer "high tech" or "agriculture." I answered, "Ransoming the captives." This is in fact a religious injunction *(pidyon ha shvuim)* found in the Torah, and it is Israel's very raison d'être. We have witnessed this principle in practice numerous times: the rescue of the hostages in the airport in Uganda; the transport of 15,000 Ethiopian Jews in a single day, which resembled the crossing of the Red Sea; and the resettlement of hundreds of thousands of Russians, both Jews and many Gentiles has been unsurpassed in modern history.

So much for the ingathering; what everybody's waiting for is the transformation. I have repeated a little maxim a thousand times: "All Jews are crazy, and this is the hospital." Not one person in a thousand has ever responded, "Hey, speak for yourself; *I'm* not crazy." A fellow reservist guarding with me last year in the prison camp replied, "Yes, but there is improvement." On the other hand, another person, who came from Germany, the daughter of Holocaust survivors, felt that there was no improvement. But nobody has disputed the premise.

That all Jews are crazy, from the trauma of rejection or from denial of it, from persecution or from assimilation, has been a tenet of Zionism from the beginning, or else why the stated need to create a home in order to achieve *normalization*? Theodore Hertzl was referred to a psychiatrist by his friends and family when he began expounding his ideas for a Jewish state. The doctor, Max Nordau, instead of curing him, became his disciple and later, as Hertzl's successor, served as the President of the Second Jewish Congress. The sickness, according their diagnosis, was assimilation. And yet, now that the political state has been established, and the recovery, optimistically speaking, is in process, we can argue over what constitutes normality - or if, indeed, it is our destiny to be normal.

But how can I go on pontificating about Zionism without at least mentioning my own case. I am a refugee, a ransomed captive, not of the political ilk perhaps, but of the criminal ilk. The crime for which I am wanted in the United States is not a felony but a misdemeanor; nevertheless, it carries with it a mandatory jail term. To the best of my knowledge, there is no extradition. I looked it up at the Yale University law library before I left. I simply decided that instead of serving a few months, at most a year's time, which would cover the criminal aspect, and possibly spending the rest of my life in involuntary, white collar servitude to cover the fines and interest, I would opt for a fresh slate in the only country on earth where I would not be an exile, but would in fact be coming out of exile. This was an experiment to determine if a positive act could counterbalance a chain of negative ones. Or, to put it in more practical terms, debt has often served in history as an inducement to emigrate. Not all the initial settlers on American shores were Puritans.

It was on the first day of Passover, 1988 that the Criminal Investigation Division of the Internal Revenue Service received my file for failure to file income tax. Two days later, I was on the plane, finally fulfilling the solemn pledge renewed every year at the seder table: "Next year in Jerusalem." How did I land up in such a pickle? Since this is not a novel but rather an essay, I will file the short form, so to speak. I will begin by throwing up my hands and saying I have no excuse. I am not innocent; I am no Alfred Dreyfuss. It was not the external impetus of anti-Semitism which drove me beyond the pale of society and its rules, but rather the corollary, the internal disease of assimilation which possibly played a part. Assimilation is a natural impulse, as natural as making love, which is, after all, its prime mover. *"And the people began to commit whoredom with the daughters of ..."* is a constant refrain in the Bible. That is why the "hedge around the law," the encyclopedic, self-referential system of oral law, was developed, to avoid succumbing to such natural impulses. That is why, for hundreds of years, Jews wore beanies, even though it is commanded neither in Torah nor Talmud. It was a mnemonic device, a reminder, both to oneself and to others that one was different. My father took off his beanie, I don't know exactly when; perhaps when he came to America from Poland at age thirteen. I don't blame him; I would have done the same. Perhaps he took it off when he joined the army during W.W.II, or perhaps he never wore one. I don't know because my father never talked about anything that ever happened to him before the age of thirteen, and about very little that happened to him until he married my mother. My mother, on the other hand, had never set foot inside a synagogue until her wedding day. It was not a mixed-marriage, but, pretty close to it in those days when, to paraphrase Rudyard Kipling, Brooklyn was Brooklyn and the Bronx was the Bronx, and never the twain shall meet. They set about establishing a nuclear family in the middle of the baby boom, a boy and a girl, both of our names beginning with the same first letter - a matched pair. We were brought up Jewish, but the main religion was Americanism, practiced and preached with the unquestioning conviction of the convert, now a self-made man. My mother, on the other hand, celebrated a variant of Americanism called consumerism, but what wasn't there to consume, a couple of Depression kids starting from nothing.

So far, a typical story, but that is why I chose to include it in essay form, as opposed to a novel. The very typicality is the *point*. Tolstoy's premise was wrong when he penned the famous opening sentence of *Anna Karenina:* "All happy families are alike." It is all *unhappy* families that are alike, as they fall into the same traps ad infinitum. The very essence of tragedy is its predictability, its inevitability. The audience wants to shout at the actors, "Don't be such a damned fool. Look out or you'll get it in the last act." Traditionally, tragedy served to moralize, to prove that the "powers that be" could not be trifled with. Of course, in our post-modernist, post moralistic age, tragedy is no longer created, because today it's only a matter of options. Instead of jumping off a cliff in a double suicide, the soap opera hero goes off with his lover, his half-sister. Screw society, or as the lyricist to *"That's Entertainment"* put it: "No more deal like the end of Camille."

Suffice it to say that I chose the option of exile, or coming out of exile, depending on one's point of view. (I will confine myself to my own case in this modest object lesson, and leave my alliterative sister, and also my other sister out of it.) When I was growing up, the idea of opting out of the American system was an inconceivable heresy. All American schoolchildren were required to read the short story, "The Man Without a Country," which depicted the despair of a traitor who had forsaken his homeland and was doomed to live, beyond hope or repentance, abroad.

All this changed in the 1960's. Before that time, evil was outside, foreign. We all knew about slavery and Lincoln's assassination and McCarthyism, but these were temporary aberrations in a basically benign system. The sixties changed all that, beginning with the Kennedy assassination. Suddenly, nobody believed the authorized version anymore. People began speculating about conspiracy theories of all kinds, and groups with opposing theories began violently opposing one another. There have been lots of articles, books, and films about this era, and I do not intend to remain on this topic, but I am a product of the sixties. Catholic, in the sense of pandemic, Americanism was put on notice as surely as if the articles had been nailed on the door of Wittenberg Cathedral. The Protestant era had begun. As a consequence, many of my generation refused to fight an undeclared war, prolonged by two corrupt administrations, both driven out of office, and America lost its first war.

I am alluding to this period in recent history for three reasons: first of all, it was instrumental in driving me to Israel; second, the crisis of faith in Zionism today parallels America's crisis of faith, though, as in many other things, Israel lags America by about thirty years; and third, it is interesting to note the role played by Jews in the youth culture and revolution of that time as compared with the behavior of young Jews of a generation before. Let us begin with the third point. In the years leading up to W.W.II, anti-Semitism in the US was so endemic that Jewish people would bend over backwards to show that their primary identity, indeed loyalty, was towards America. This was so much so that Jewish leaders, such as the great Reform leader, Rabbi Stephen Wise, actually lobbied the Roosevelt administration *not* to increase immigration quotas from the very countries Jews were trying to flee in panic. They were demonstrating that they were Americans first. Furthermore, a flood of folk with beards and beanies would not improve the situation for the loyal, clean-shaven ranks of the Mosaic persuasion. This quiet lobbying continued right into the 1940's. This fact has been well documented in the book, *The Deafening Silence/American Jewish Leaders and the Holocaust* by Rafael Medoff (May 1986 Carol Pub Group; ISBN: 0933503636)   Perhaps this is why the Holocaust is such a fetish with American Jews today, to assuage guilty consciences over their sin of omission, the failure to protest at that fateful time. Of course this would be most vehemently denied.

Nor does it detract from the military contribution of many American Jews. But by and large, the name of the game was "Don't Make Waves."

One generation later, it was Bob Dylan who popularized the protest song, Abbie Hoffman and Jerry Rubin who led the Yippies, Carl Alpert, who along with Timothy Leary, led in experimentation with LSD, and millions of Jewish kids who were actively challenging the system. Of course the counter-culture was not composed only of Jews, perhaps not even the majority, but the ratio was very high. Perhaps we now felt secure enough to complain about the service, without fear of being thrown out of the hotel, or accused of dual loyalty or, worse, treason like the Rosenbergs. This new feeling of belonging may have been overly sanguine, but still, what turned out to be the reformation, instead of revolution, of the sixties did do a lot to curb overt racism.

As to my own case, my Song of Ascents, which was more a series of descents leading to the immolation of my former identity and my regathering to the bosom of my people in the Promised Land, here are a few landmarks: After my Bar Mitzvah in 1962 followed by a celebration which, in keeping with the times, resembled a mini-Camelot, I curtailed my Jewish education. We had moved, after the recent birth of my second sister, to a big house on the other side of town, away from the development of garden apartments called Beacon Hill (after the prestigious, and probably restricted, area of Boston) but which even some of us kids jokingly called Kike's Peak," where we had lived since leaving the Bronx. I was the only Jew in my new circle of friends, but it was not for that reason that I felt myself an outsider. My best friend in high school favored both the politics and rhetorical style of William F. Buckley, now an elder statesman of Conservatism, and the histrionic operas of Richard Wagner. He also knew judo, to my detriment, and his constant sparring sooner or later ended my friendship with him and all of his local constituents.

When it came time to go away to college, I chose the one which was furthest away from home, and where nobody was going who knew me. I went through fraternity rush and, despite the fact that I perceived myself as both handsome and witty, I received only one invitation to pledge. I did not realize it at the time, but the fraternity I pledged was 100% Jewish. After six months I quit, convincing others to de-pledge along with me. The ostensible reason was our objection to "hazing," particularly the verbal abuse heaped on one blindfolded boy. But the real reason was that I had been drawn into another fraternity, the fraternity of hippies or pot-heads, or freaks, as we called ourselves. This fellowship was in no way restricted; we were all misfits, though of course, like in any other group, there was a hierarchy here, too. I was near the top of the hierarchy by virtue of the fact that I was the roommate of the campus drug dealer. That meant that much of the "action" took place in or near my room. This was my first brush with criminality. We lived under the assumption that our phone was bugged. At political demonstrations, which were beginning to become common, we suspected that we were photographed by the F.B.I.; it turned out many were. I was only taken aback when my roommate announced that he would, if necessary, kill a narc.

Looking back, it is interesting that, in a university that probably had a Jewish quota, I figure that, conservatively speaking, at least 75% of the freaks were Jews. It has now been almost thirty years since I saw most of my college friends, but the last I heard, one was in a mental institution for proclaiming himself Michael the Archangel (Catholic), one joined the cult of Indian so-called avatar Maher Baba, who coined the expression, "Don't Worry, Be Happy" on buttons with his grinning face. At least one came out of the closet. One put down his guitar and became a real estate developer in San Francisco, so truly I cannot claim, like the narrator of *Moby Dick* echoing Job's messenger that "I alone am left to tell." By another accounting I may not have been left to tell, but disappeared to another shore under an assumed name.

After college, I spent close to a year living alone on my parents' newly purchased country estate, writing my first novel (subsequently burned in a fit of religious ecstasy) concerning those college years and my first romance. (Only once did I ever go out with a Jewish girl, but I soon discovered that she had recently attempted suicide, and furthermore, she was also having a relationship with another man, a black man, in the hope of having either one of our babies.) After passing a lonely winter on the idled, and as yet unrenovated farm, I decided to return to the area where I had attended college, specifically to the town where my college girlfriend had come from, hoping to bump into her once again. In order to accomplish this, I called a friend, a woman who lived in the same exclusive suburb. I simply called her and said, "I would like to visit you for three weeks or longer," without telling her my ulterior motive. The visit lasted sixteen years.

We were married four years after my arrival, after numerous partings and reconciliations which had dragged us back and forth, and coast to coast like yo-yo's. We were married in a Baptist Church which I found in the Yellow Pages. Only her family attended. The pastor's wife played the only hymn I knew at the time, *"I'll Fly Away,"* a self-fulfilling prophecy which would have been more appropriate to a funeral. I was her second Jewish husband, and I was induced by her to fight the first, a man who was old enough to be my father. She was thirteen years my senior.

She had a way of expressing herself that was more expressive, more piquant and more bombastic than American English. That is because she was not American born. She was born and raised in Serbia, and yes, we did relive the Balkan Wars over and over involving the Orthodox Serbs, Croatian Catholics, and Moslems, whom she called Turks. She, having come out of the Second World War emotionally scarred, was the closest thing to a survivor I could find. She claimed to love Jews, claimed even that her family were "righteous gentiles," a technical term that Israel uses in honoring those who risked their lives to help Jews in Europe during the war. This was an exaggeration. (There was a family acquaintance, a Jew, whom I later met, who hid with the same underground faction, the royalists, largely discredited at the time and later as having been obstructionists.) At other times she claimed to *be* a Jew, first, speculating about some possible ancestor and later embracing the cult of British Israelism which claims that the Celts are the lost tribes of Israel. She went one step further by speculating that the Slavic Serbian tribe was actually an offshoot of the Celts who stayed behind in their westward migration. The point is that *most* anti-Semites in some way actually identify with the Jews in order that they may replace us.

I have skipped over the whole Oedipal factor, bumping off a father figure, a psychiatrist no less. It was to fight him with his own weapons that she had undergone psychoanalysis and then had laid into his Brooklyn Jewish upbringing, particularly his mother, whom she slandered as a coat-hanger abortionist while professing love. I, on the other hand, was characterized as the son of "merchants" to whom everything, including love, was reduced to a pound of flesh.

Having now swung from Bar Mitzvah Boy in Blue, making my entrance into the festive hall, arm in arm with aforementioned alliterative sister, to radical hippie arrested at the occupation of the campus ROTC, it was time to grab the nearest vine heading back in the opposite direction. I became a born-again Christian. I crossed over the line, went beyond the bounds. Emulation was one thing, participation another. We are dealing with boundaries here. I am one of those organisms that tested them. I didn't go from Jew to Christian in a single bound; I was not instantaneously translated into a state of gentility. In fact, I opted for the radical fringe, the "charismatic" non-denominational denomination. After all, weren't the Jewish founders of Christianity a radical fringe? We could outprotest the Protestants, be purer than the Puritans. I rejected all vestiges of paganism, including Sunday, Christmas, Easter, and all birthdays (which I later learned are also shunned by Jehovah's Witnesses). Everything was tainted. Everything must be restored to its roots. I didn't then realize that the Jewish month of Tammuz, and possibly most of the others, are named after Babylonian gods.

It was at this time that the backlash of right-wing, fundamentalism was finding a political agenda. School prayer had been abolished, abortion legalized, and a vocal minority called the "Moral Majority," along with scores of other organizations, spurred on by evangelist broadcasters, were fighting back, to return America to the "Christian nation" it never really was. Of course it was always home to a majority of Christians, but from the beginning, there were also proponents of the Enlightenment, Deists, who would today be called agnostics, Masons, and, as mentioned, debtors and outlaws. Our children were sent to parochial schools, often one room affairs, where they would not be subjected to the conspiracy of "secular humanism." Permissiveness was out. At one home fellowship we attended, led by a couple barely in their twenties who specialized in leading sailors in the brig into dramatic conversions, children were expected to remain sitting silently for hours on end while their parents waved their rods of correction to and fro as if they were swatting flies.

Now, by no means do I mean to infer that my religious convictions led me to transgress the law. Conformity to the law was encouraged. Nevertheless, the government was in enemy hands. The belief that the world was ruled by an evil cartel of power hungry money-men, foremost among them the Rothschilds, was preached in many churches and published in numerous books. That the Federal Reserve and its chief architect, German Jew Jacob Schiff, who also laid the groundwork for federal income tax, were in on this conspiracy, I also heard and read repeatedly. It was all preparing for the Antichrist and the coming Armageddon. That this theory was a reissue of the libelous "Protocols of the Elders of Zion," first promulgated at the turn of the century in Czarist Russia and resurfacing in Nazi Germany, and again in the publications of the John Birch Society, and again in Japanese cults, and again in certain Arab countries, I did not then realize.

So, when the Criminal Investigation Division of the Internal Revenue Service received my file, I had not only been turning over a lot of currency on Wall Street, where I had taken my place as an "honest broker," but I had been turning over a lot of propaganda as well. Meanwhile,
we pissed away all the money, going from coast to coast and at

least twelve residences in as many years. I would estimate that my wife and I did not share the same abode, let alone the same bed, roughly half the time. And those were the circumstances under which I arrived in Israel.

I spent my first year writing another book (also to remain unpublished). I did publish one thing, however, a poster which I hawked on the promenade in Jerusalem known as Ben Yehuda, but which I call the New Via Delarosa because it is lined with all types of fringe characters singing for their supper in all the tongues of men and, possibly, angels. So, I became a publisher, much more my line than power hungry money-man. Also, that first year, I met my second wife. My first one refused to divorce me and now, seven years later, the High Court in Jerusalem has finally assigned jurisdiction to a local court, and so my marriage is to be dissolved.

One morning, seven years ago, when I was occupying a bunk at one of the youth hostels in Jerusalem, I got into a conversation with a new acquaintance, one of the shadowy characters with no visible means of support who drift in and out of Jerusalem on spiritual quests. This man, we'll call him Duane, was occupying a bunk in the small cell set aside for long term residents. He was still, after ten years, recovering from his first marriage. His wife had left him for his best friend. Shortly afterward, he had lost his job as pastor of a well-to-do congregation, and ever since, he had renounced material possessions, actually burying his last mementos, including his wedding ring, in a hole in Jerusalem, and had hopped between there and California while awaiting his call, or more precisely, recall to the ministry. Among the other resident ascetics were an old man who believed that he had discovered the true site of Mount Sinai, not on the peninsula of that name, but, he conceded after much prodding, in the Negev, probably not far from where I am stationed now, an outpost called both then and now Kadesh. Another bunk was occupied by a middle-aged hipster, ex-Madison Avenue executive, in a knitted yarmulke who, during his lengthy stay completed and published a short pamphlet consisting of twenty lines on the subject of dying, which he did soon after.

The fourth bunk was granted to a man who received it along with his board in return for janitorial services. He was a smart aleck, despite what was clearly a subnormal IQ Or perhaps he simply lacked communication skills; he spoke so fast that only his roommates could understand him. In all, these men lived as monks, with all the eccentricities of monks.

"Do you want to know what my name was in the States?" I asked Duane that morning over a breakfast of diced cucumber and tomato salad, white cheese, bread and chocolate spread, which constitutes the unvarying breakfast menu in second, but not third rate hostels.

"Sure"

I explained to him how my last name had had the connotation, in its original Yiddish, of restlessness, of not being able to sit still. Now, I had taken my own Jewish name and added my father's first name, the one he had been named in Poland and had therefore never mentioned. I only learned it when he was called to the Torah at my Bar Mitzvah. So, in effect, the meaning of my name had been changed from literally "pins" with the connotation of "ants in the pants" to literally, "life in the shadow of God." Also Bezalel, my father's, and now my namesake was the artist in the Bible who carried out the designs for the ark and the tabernacle. I was trying to make my friend understand that for me, coming to Israel, regardless of the circumstances, represented the restoration and normalization of my true self.

The next morning he came down to breakfast with his diary. "Didn't we meet in Denny's Restaurant in Santa Monica, California on May 18, 1981?" he asked. I am estimating the time and place of our introduction by a mutual friend, but doubtless, his diary was accurate.

"And I told you that I'd probably move to Israel," I remembered.

"And I told you I might see you there."

Now we come to the question of fate, or kismet, or bashert, or destiny, or providence, or the finger of God. I recently received a letter from a rabbi whom I never met, remarking upon another coincidence. He was my first mail order customer.

Replying to our address printed in a package of greeting cards which we publish he had not known that I had grown up in his town, become Bar Mitzvah in his synagogue years before his arrival. "Conscience is God's way of remaining anonymous," he wrote in answer to my informing him of my other identity. I wrote back, "True; so is coincidence." The reply came: "Spell Check didn't catch that on my computer. I meant coincidence."

It was through the coincidence of running into Duane, a casual acquaintance, that I met my second wife, Yonnah. First she married him. As a favor to him I was the photographer at their wedding. But actually it wasn't a real wedding at all. I say this as a statement of fact, not out of any bad feelings whatsoever. It was a fiction, and now there is nothing left of it; even my brilliant photographs were destroyed. The reason why the wedding was not real was that in Israel, a Jew and a gentile cannot be married. They can marry elsewhere, and they did, the next week in Cyprus, but the ceremony which took place on the Mount of Olives, overlooking the Old City on a cloudless September day, the ceremony arranged by my wife with the assent of her shadow husband and presided over by at least three ordained ministers, not including the one she married, was only a play because, in the final analysis, none of them had the power vested in them by the state to pronounce them man and wife. And so, when everything unraveled right from the beginning, during the dual purpose civil ceremony-honeymoon in Cyprus, (birthplace, as my wife pointed out, of Aphrodite, *her* previous namesake in one of its derivations), it was no surprise. The groom did not, after all, wish to be married.

At the same time it was becoming clear that my wife was not coming with our children, as we had planned. and also, as I was finally admitting to myself, I didn't want her to come. Meanwhile, I was becoming friendly with the abandoned bride. After all, we had so much in common. Each of our spouses had hoped to ride onto Mount Zion, if not on an ass, then at least on the coattails of one. (Mine insisted she would live nowhere else.)

She was getting "counseling" from one of the pastoral triumvirate and his wife - Baptists. Their advice: Hold on to the absent husband. Even when he left right after the honeymoon and installed himself in a Catholic monastery on the Sea of Galilee. And then they continued with the same exhortation after he left the country. When, several months later I gave up my apartment and moved in with her, we were publicly disfellowshipped from the pulpit, the Protestant equivalent of excommunication.

And so began our road to normalization, if you will. Shortly afterwards, we left Jerusalem and moved to Ashkelon by the sea, and after a while joined a synagogue, not a religious one. We were not asked to renounce the devil and his works. For us, normalization is living in a country whose borders are not recognized, affiliating with a synagogue which is not recognized in that country. We were so earnest when we met that we would have married right away, and thus I would have lost half of my subsidies. Thank God he protects the feebleminded. We were both sick and we wanted to get better.

She was a close to a *shiksa* as I could find. Her father's ancestors arrived in Virginia in the late 1600's from England. She had been brought up in a wealthy, largely Jewish area near Seattle, not knowing that she was a Jew. Her mother's family came over from Germany in the early nineteenth century, among the first Jews to settle in America. Of that side of the family, only a fraction have remained Jewish. Her mother, a beauty, died at age 21, shortly after giving birth. At age 16 Yonnah was informed by her father that her mother had been Jewish. It was after coming to Israel, on a visit, that she was told that if her mother was Jewish then she was Jewish, and could immigrate according to the Law of Return (which actually requires only a Jewish grandparent). So wee have both been different people with different names, nor do we hide our secret identities.

Several years ago, I heard on the radio an obituary for Jerry Segal, the man who created the comic book character, *Superman*. It was interesting to discover that the cartoonist was a Jew who came of age in the 1940's. The Superman saga is about alter-egos, dual identities, heroes and anti-heroes and finally, about assimilation. An alien resident from an ancient civilization, he must pose as a wimp, behind thick glasses and conventional attire to disguise his real identity. Although he loves Lois Lane, he avoids intermarriage with her. He never reveals his true identity Above all, he secretly longs to be normal, to blend in, but he cannot abandon his high, almost Messianic calling. Though originally from another planet (ancient Israel), he was brought up in Smallville (the shtetle), lives in cosmopolitan Metropolis (New York City) and works for the internationalist Daily Planet. Superman is the alter-ego of the assimilated Jew. His dreamlike ability to fly, in fact he exhibits the basic protective devices of both fight and flight. He is the Golem, that fictional, metaphysical, dreamlike creation from Jewish folklore - superhuman protector of the helpless and weak. And even as the Golem was created through the secret Kabbalistic utterance of the explicit name of God and made to appear or disappear through the combination of letters, the letters that combine to spell the word "man" in Hebrew, so one of Superman's nemeses, a trickster from a parallel dimension, can be made to depart only by saying his unpronounceable name backwards.

What then is the source of abnormality for the Jew? It is the lack of clear and defined boundaries. Just as a person needs to be individuated, even by the mere possession of an address, so does a people. There are only two places on earth where Jews are more than guests, however enfranchised they may be. Many Zionists would say that there is only one place, Israel, and that is that. But there is a polyglot country, ethnically and religiously pluralistic, owing no allegiance to race or nationality or commonwealth or king. That country is, of course, the United States, the alternative haven. Furthermore, no other country in the world represents freedom to the extent of America. The price of this freedom, of course, is assimilation, if not in one generation, then, at most, in three. Not since Hellenism set out to assimilate the world 2300 years ago, has such a dominant acculturating force existed. All the world wants to be free, in Levi's bluejeans like the Marlboro Man. Israel, of course, is not exempt. The problem is, we may be a small country, but we've got several bona fide religions to contend with, and this does not necessarily facilitate the uninhibited expression of freedom. The Minister of Culture suggests that we retire the God of Hosts and adopt the Nine Muses as our mascots. To be fair, she was making a play on words since, in Hebrew, the word "hosts" can be translated "armies." But, like its Hellenic predecessor, the American influence is not monolithic, neither internally nor externally. Rather, it absorbs and standardizes, turning a simple hamburger into the platonic ideal of the hamburger.

The opening of the first McDonalds Temple of the Golden Arches in Tel Aviv was greeted with much publicity and fanfare. It was, in the eyes of the local populace, a normalizing experience. "Over 4 Billion Served," was the posted tally of hamburgers when I last noticed, before leaving America. Never, since the Temple sacrifices ceased in Jerusalem has such a careful accounting been given of braised meat. But Consumerism is not a jealous god. The shopping mall presents a uniform environment from city to city, country to country, day to day, season to season - a casino world, a sanctum sanctorum without clocks or windows; it is a world without borders.

The backlash against this homogenizing trend is the erection of artificial borders, the taking on of the veil in order to insulate the group from the outside world. This always involves the promulgation of an increasingly complex set of rules and regulations. Militancy can be internalized or externalized. Not many centuries ago, Christian soldiers were marching onward not "*as to war*" as is sung in the hymn, but to actual religious wars. And in Israel today there are calls, albeit from a minority, for the reinstatement of religious law mandated by Constitution. It is interesting to note that when America became a theocracy, for a short time in the late 1600's, they soon began burning witches in Salem. The separation of religion and state is also a question of borders.

For the past few centuries, from the "Age of Enlightenment" until recently, the Western world has relegated religion to the status of myth. It may be interesting, it may be uplifting, but it is fiction; and even if we may suspend our disbelief, as we do in order to appreciate fiction, it is not real in any verifiable way.

We believe that we live in a secular age, with firm lines of demarcation between matters secular and religious. The modern trend toward secularization and the avowed separation of religion and state still brings about religious parties or religious movements within political parties because, on a deep level, religion underlies politics. Furthermore, any orthodoxy, even secular humanism, is a form of religion. This thought is anathema to the "liberal" mind, which believes that even if it were true, it would be better not to think about it; sooner or later in our evolution, it will fall away like our tails. If there were no borders between religion and politics, then all wars would be religious wars, wars of annihilation.

When the Temple Mount was captured in 1967, secular soldiers wept along with religious ones. But such strong feelings were quickly repressed. Even though Jewish synagogues and gravestones had been turned into stables and latrines by our enemies, the keys to the Temple Mount were soon relinquished. No one wanted a religious war, not realizing that nearly all wars are religious wars - witness Afghanistan, Bosnia, Chechnia, and Northern Ireland in this decade, or the perverse pagan brand of millenialism of the Third Reich fifty years ago, and of course all of Israel's wars with the Arabs. Thus, the Dome of the Rock sits upon a Byzantine church, which sits upon a Roman temple which sits on the Temple Mount. Our Minister of Culture has a point. It is still a *gotterdamerung*, a war among the gods. Even World War I, a war almost universally acknowledged as having been caused by nationalism, can been seen as having religious roots. This illustration is so far off the beaten track of conventional interpretations, that it cannot be left unsubstantiated:

The Serbian victory in the Second Balkan War of June-July 1913 was a grave disappointment to Austria-Hungary, the last vestige of the Holy Roman Empire. Already in 1913, Austria-Hungary had been threatening to attack Serbia. Austrian Prince Schonburg visited the Vatican and sent the following report on November 3, 1913 to his Minister of Foreign Affairs, Count Berchtold, reporting on the conversations that he was carrying on there with the Pope and his Secretary of State :

"Among the first subjects tackled by the Cardinal Secretary of State during our interview last week, as was to be expected, was the question of Serbia. The Cardinal began by expressing his joy at the energetic and commendable attitude we have recently adopted. During today's audience (upon which I have made a separate report, see Document A) His Holiness, who began the interview by mentioning the energetic steps we have taken at Belgrade, made several very characteristic remarks. 'Certainly,' then said His Holiness, 'Austria-Hungary would have done better to punish the Serbs for all the mistakes that have been made.'"2

One day after the outbreak of what was to become World War I, on July 29, 1914, the Austrian Charge d'Affaires at the Vatican sent the following dispatch to his superior, the same Count Berchtold: "When, two days ago, I went to the Cardinal Secretary of State *(of the Vatican)*, he did, of course, speak about the serious questions and problems that at present preoccupy the whole of Europe. His Eminence's conversation bore no sign of any apparent goodwill or moderation. He unreservedly approved the note *(ultimatum)* addressed to Serbia, and he indirectly expressed hope that the monarchy would hold out to the end. 'It goes without saying,' remarked the Cardinal, 'that it is regrettable that Serbia should not have been brought low a long time ago.' This declaration is equally consonant with the Pope's opinion: many a time during the past year His Holiness has expressed his regret that Austria-Hungary should have missed the opportunity to subdue its Danubian neighbor.'"3 Thus, the Hapsburg Empire, along with its allies, was to serve as the secular arm to annihilate the influence of Eastern Orthodoxy emanating from Russia and the Balkans and to preserve the power of the Roman Catholic Church in the region. *(Scholars in Israel can find these documents in the National Library in Jerusalem.)*

I give this example only to show that what is generally viewed as secular history in a secularist century, can also be also viewed as religious history. I could have chosen many other examples from modern history. For example, after the Second World War, certain elements of the Japanese religion of Shintoism were dismantled, particulary emperor worship. In other words, scratch politics, and you'll often find religion. This is even more obvious in our post-modernist age, when the limits of rationalism have been ascertained, and religious revivalism, for better or worse, is on the rise. This is largely due to the artificial barriers which had been dividing various fields of human affairs. The search for holiness is a search for wholeness or holism in the face of fragmentation. But once we put the pie back together, the question becomes, who gets the pie?

Let us then look at Jerusalem, not as a pie, to be apportioned slice by slice, nor as a pie in the sky to suddenly descend upon us with an incontestable trumpet blast, but rather as a seven layer cake. When King Hussein recently flew over, tipping his wings above the lavishly re-gilded Dome of the Rock, he was signifying his custodianship of the cherry on top of the cake. When Arafat declared *jihad* over Jerusalem, shortly after signing a treaty with Israel, he was trying to have his cake and eat it, too. And when the ultra-orthodox burial society, *hevrat hakadisha*, demonstrates against archaeologists whom they accuse of disturbing ancient Jewish graves, they are trying to make sure that the plate on which the cake sits is kosher. So, it is not as easy as two-dimensional pie. It is a three dimensional grid, four counting the element of time. The problem is a calculus, not an algebraic equation, that is if the problem is solvable at all.

We are living in an era where symbol supersedes fact; and whenever symbols become confused with facts, the sword becomes confused with the pen. The Crusaders' quest for the Holy Grail, the mythical chalice of the Last Supper, was such a bloody confusion.

In the distance, Bedouin maidens herd goats. Do they maintain their nomadic life across borders. I observe them through the binoculars, as they wave their sticks, bringing back a stray. Beneath black burnooses they wear colorful fabrics. Egyptian officers ride by on camels, while pairs of enlisted men trudge in the sand carrying canteens and calling over to us for water and girlie magazines. We are at peace. The scanty fence is all that separates two worlds, the Third World from whichever one we inhabit. We are only a few miles from the prison camp where I stood guard last winter.

There, I was completely stripped of my bearings. Prison is another experience devoid of clocks or windows. I remember my arrival at that eerie destination. I had been given leave to arrive one day late, as long as I found my own way. The rest of my unit had been transported by bus from our base near Tel Aviv. I took a regular bus to Beersheva in time to make the connection for the last trip to Ketziot, which I had been told was my station. However, we arrived late in Beersheva, so I missed my connection. I went in to the dispatcher's office to see if there was another bus, and met a group of young people who had also missed the bus. They had a party in Nitzana, on the Egyptian border. The dispatcher suggested that we share a taxi. It was about midnight when the taxi dropped me off at Ketziot junction. The driver was not sure where the prison was located, so I walked toward some lights on the horizon. The only sound was my footsteps as I approached the lights, until I began to hear the distinctive sounds of a prison- the shouts of prisoners in the prison yard, the commands barked over the loudspeaker, each announcement introduced by a siren. By now the entire area before me was lit up as bright as day. When I arrived at the gate, I was told that my unit was not there; perhaps they were stationed at another prison, several kilometers down the road. I returned to the road, but decided to save time by cutting across the field. I hoped I wouldn't be shot by mistake in the rock strewn desert. Finally, I arrived at the prison, and the soldiers there knew where my unit was. They drove me there in a truck, to Prison Number Seven.

When I think of it, every one of my postings has been an exercise in coping with disorientation. The previous year, when I was stationed on the highest peak in Judea, the freak blizzard was so heavy that the drifts were over our heads and our replacements couldn't make it to the base, causing us to serve extra time. The year before that, I had done my basic training at age forty, during the Gulf War. Our trainers were kids half my age, and they were more nervous than we. Finally, I volunteered with several others for guard duty at an isolated encampment, also in the Judean wilderness. Here we slept in tents and did our patrols on foot, wandering around the hills, seeing antelope, flocks of sheep, and sometimes, at night, a scud, looking like a shooting star leaving a trail on its way to more populated areas. In times like these, when the routine of civilian life is invaded, when the rhythm of day and night is arbitrarily broken up by spells of guard duty, we feel like sleepwalkers. Like the brainwashed, through fatigue, monotony and the disappearance of normal boundaries that define our lives, our defense mechanisms break down; the unconscious comes to the fore. That is why friendships formed in the army are unique. Sooner or later, all the secrets come out. This is why I took up pen and camera - because the territories herein recorded are also interior, that is internal. And finally, this is the last frontier - the reconciliation of the interior and exterior worlds we inhabit.

1.*Jerusalem Post*, May 12, 1995, A View From Nov, quoting article in *Yerushaliyim*, April 28, 1995
2. Document P.A. XI/291, Diplomatic Archives of Austria
3. Veroffentlichungen der Kommission fur neuere Geschichte Osterrichs, 26 Wien-Liepzig 1930, p. 893

In the distance Bedouin maidens herd goats.

Border Patrol

When I was young,
(that unincorporated state
which once stretched before me like the prairie –
pristine, seemingly endless frontier,
since disappeared, plowed under
with no possibility of regeneration or return)
I was an advocate of borders.
They were part of my individuation,
providing the stamp of experience,
when symbol superseded substance,
and a full passport indicated a life lived
or at least set foot in.
Then I passed through the Age of Revolution,
and I didn't like them anymore.
We wanted to storm all the barricades
Chanting "Solidarity Forever"
when they rounded us up in the paddywagon.
Of course those who reject borders
soon find themselves confined to very small spaces
(in my case a small nation
whose borders are presently under negotiation).
Also in the disposition of love,
I have learned not to squander my natural resources,
but rather to embark upon a gradual process
of mutual recognition.
(Sometimes the body politic is aroused
to a firm raising of the colors;
this often leads to joint exercises,
total engagement, and full bilateral relations.)

In the Public Domain

Manifest Destiny

One must
wonder how the railroad
Divided the buffalo
Until it hits one like an iron horse:
Immovable object meeting
Irresistable force –
Another bison bisected
Bites the dust.

Gilgamesh (revisited)

Apotheosis of blood and earth
      transfiguration, substantiation
Do you read me?
This is the Age of Implosion
emptiness inside, pressure from without.
Images remixed, old songs revived
      it's all been said before -
Another Balkan War revised
      it's all been said before -
on the black box
May Day May Day
surface connections, genuflections
      to the great mother goddess whore
in her myriad manifestations
      healer and destroyer, consort
of wine besotted Gilgamesh god.
The message has gone to the uttermost
      ends of the earth
so every johnny people is a chosen brood,
Or by the same token, if all are, no one is.

For Yonnah

Israel is the desire of the world.
That's why everyone wants to possess her.
What is the attraction
That they all swarm around like flies?
Even the shape of her,
The continents like torso and buttocks
And arms and legs wrapped around.
She is skinny as a crack,
But inside is every earthly delight.
She must not be taken by force,
For her father is very jealous
And he never sleeps.
Only by undying love, love strong as death,
Will she yield her fruits.
Her passion is very deep,
And though it contains a sea of salt tears,
Yet it has been changed to sweetness and joy,
Only the marshes left for salt.
So long have I wandered,
And she has walked through the valley of the shadow.
I will comfort her and rejoice in her.
When shall the times of the Gentiles be fulfilled
So I can fully enter in
And drink of the fountain of waters
Gushing from the flint rock?
All her fault lines, like nerves,
Converge in her capital—
A very sensitive spot.

—*Jerusalem, 1989*

Pilgrim's Redress

This is the land
of broken dreams
and broken words
which lie like shards
on stones and sand
And nothing's ever
as it seems.
This is the land
at the end of the quest
This is the land
of eternal unrest,
of shattering truth
and shattering lies.
This is the land
where illusion dies.

Isaac and Rebecca

Sweet Betsy
had no more pikes to seek
She was up the creek.
Poor Betsy
crossed the sea
to an ancient land
where it all began
in the sands of time.
It's a hard life
for the wife
of the likes of Ike
who likes to hike
on Blind Man's Bluff
and play hide and seek
on the mountain peak
like Abraham and
the ram in the bramble.

Jerusalem and Tel Aviv Compared

City of stone.
City of sand.
City of gold.
City of tan.
City of visions and isms,
Divisions and schisms.
City of white light,
And city of prisms.

View From My Window

Like the dove returned
I see the tips of olive trees.
Their leaves flicker and glimmer
in the wind like silver coins
And so I find harmony
after the deluge.

I am drunk on the cultivation,
not of the vine, but of the rose bush.
Their flowers, wet with dew
Assuage my sadness
At so much left behind
And so many rivers left to cross.
In my abstraction
I see the symmatry
of the stately palm
Dripping cornucopias
of fruit among the fronds.
I am ready to face my Anakim.*

*Anakim are giants

City of visions and isms

Divisions and schisms

Workaday Verse

Ode to Commerce

Blessed are the salesmen
who apotheosize the product,
the tangible manifestation, the thing –
who rhapsodize in borrowed feathers,
buyers and sellers both.
Antithesis of sloth, they wait, they pursue,
as those who slew the wooly mammoth
or gathered non-hybrid seed, primitive corn -
which is what they dispense in one form or another.
They bring stability to our breed.
Yet e'en there be a sucker born a minute,
how great a faith to persevere in his solicitation.
Needless to examples cite, the world is full
Of items quite adequately heralded.

Hack

This is a 100% recycled poem.
The delicate equalibrium of the earth
has not been disturbed by draining
precious mental resources.
It's all been said anyhow.
We cater to the popular market -
A ditty to fit every purse.
Our marketing research indicates
An unsaturated demand for
easy listening verse.
Every poem is lovingly assembled
by our staff.
(Poetic license provided upon request.)

Song of Degrees

The bankers round about me said
Cut him off from staff and bread
But God my portion was abiding
To Jerusalem I went riding
On the bus with one-way fare
Trusting that when I got there
I would my credit so extend
That I could then ride home again.

The Unknown Poet

I am a working poet
I sweat and toil 'tis true
If you havent go a penny
A ha'penny will do.

I am a minor poet
I sing a minor key
If you haven't got a ha'penny
Then God bless me.

I am the unknown poet
No praise nor prize for prattle
Just put me in an unmarked grave
And say, "He fought the battle."

Of Justice and Equity

Daumier depicted justice
      as a bartered commodity
And yet his images hang like icons
      in lawyer's offices.
Fame is but the clapping
      of trained seals,
Religion, the revenge
      of the underdog
           in this world or the next.
Love shall remain
      in the public domain.
In all varieties, all is vanity.
Still, the preacher found
      it is best to keep busy

Bit Part

An extra in a foreign film,
only it is not the film, but I
    who am foreign.
I play an attorney, without a line -
like an armless juggler -
I only feign conversation
with my colleague on the bench
(he inevitably responds, sotto voce,
"The matter remains to be clarified."
It is summer and we sweat
    under black robes -
windows sealed with filters,
no air conditioning or whirring fan,
while each witness recounts
the unfortunate circumstances
twenty or thirty times over -
Hell for a day, with catered lunch.

This is the land of broken dreams

And nothing's ever as it seems

photo by Yonnah Ben Levy

Chaim Bezalel was born in New York City in 1949 and grew up in Dobbs Ferry. After studying film at Northwestern University, he spent several years doing photo essays. For ten years he gave up photography entirely and worked as a stockbroker. Knowing he was in trouble with the IRS for failure to file income tax for several years, he fled to Israel in 1988 (with two suitcases), resumed his photography and established an art publishing company together with new wife and artistic collaborator, Yonnah Ben Levy. Having rebuilt his live in Israel, he returned to the U.S. in 1997 to face the consequences, and served 106 days in Lewisburg Federal Prison Camp and three years probation. He and his wife now reside on Camano Island in Washington while also maintaining a home in Ashkelon, Israel. For the last two years they have been exhibiting their work coast to coast and reconnecting with family.